MAKE ME LAUGH!

GAME-DAY GIGGLERS

WINNING JOKES TO SCORE SOME LAUGHS

by Sam Schultz
pictures by Brian Gable

Carolrhoda Books, Inc. • Minneapolis

Benny: My mother told me I'm not to play football with my glasses.

Jenny: You won't have to. We're playing with a football.

Q: Why does it take longer to run from second base to third base than from first base to second base?

A: Because there's a shortstop between second and third.

Joey gave his baseball coach a jar full of flies.

Coach: What's this for?

Joey: You told me to go home and practice catching flies. Here's a jar full. I caught every one of them!

Johnny: Mom, I'm going out to play football.

Mom: With your brand new shirt?

Johnny: No, with the kids next door!

Bert: Did you ever see a catfish?

Gert: Don't kid me. Cats don't fish.

Brother: Did I tell you about the touchdown I made?

Sister: No, and I appreciate it!

Fisherman: Tell me, what do you do when you get a bite?

Girl: Scratch it.

Mary: Look at the fish I caught!

Larry: Wow! That's a big one. What are you going to do with it?

Mary: I'm going to take it home for dinner.

Fish: No thanks. I already had dinner!

Mom: What are you doing home, Jake? I thought you were at baseball practice.

Jake: I was. But I hit the ball over the fence and the manager told me to run home!

Q: Why is a batter like a horse's tail?

A: They're both flyswatters.

Jack: I ran 95 yards for a touchdown, and they kicked me off the team.

Pete: Why did they do that?

Jack: Because I ran the wrong way!

Joey: I made a 90-yard run in football today.

Tom: Hey, that's great!

Joey: Not so great. I couldn't catch the guy in front of me who had the ball!

Heather: Mom, we played baseball today, and I stole second base!

Mom: Well you march right back to school and give it back!

Q: Why don't chickens make good baseball players?

A: They can only hit fowl balls.

Uncle: What do you want to be when you grow up, Tyler?

Tyler: I want to be a tough charging lineman on a football team.

Uncle: Well, you can be sure I won't stand in your way!

Q: Why is bowling called a quiet sport?

A: Because you can always hear a pin drop.

Lisa: Did you enjoy the baseball game?

Laura: No, it reminded me of bad pancakes. Neither team had a good batter.

Owner of Lake: Young man, there's no fishing here!

Boy Fishing: You're telling me! I've been fishing here for two hours, and I haven't had a bite yet.

Leslie: Dad, remember how you always used to worry that I'd break a window when I played baseball in the backyard?

Dad: Yes, I remember.

Leslie: Well, you can stop worrying now!

Dentist: Where do your teeth ache?

Child: First row—right field.

Coach: What's the best way to hold a bat?

Player: By the wings!

Jessie: I don't play tennis because it's too noisy.

Tanya: Noisy?

Jessie: Yeah, everybody raises a racket.

Quarterback: Are you hurt?

Halfback: I think so. Better call me a doctor.

Quarterback: Okay. You're a doctor.

John: I always wear two pairs of pants when I go golfing.

Ron: Why?

John: In case I get a hole in one!

Billie: My mother went horseback riding and got a headache.

Millie: That's not where I ache when I go horseback riding!

Q: What can you serve but not eat?

A: A tennis ball.

Jimmy: My mother got a medal for racing.

Timmy: What kind of racing?

Jimmy: Raising a family!

Safari Leader: If you see a leopard, shoot him on the spot.

Hunter: There's a leopard. Quick, which spot?

Teacher: Class, who knows who defeated the Philistines?

Student: I think it was the New York Yankees.

Son: Dad, you should have seen the baseball game I saw today. The bases were loaded, the batter made a home run, and not a man scored.

Dad: How come?

Son: It was a girls' baseball team!

Q: Why is a football called a pigskin?

A: Because most football players like to "hog" the ball.

Sarah: Hey, Marcia, why aren't you wearing your baseball uniform?

Marcia: Because my doctor said I can't play baseball.

Sarah: Heck, I could have told you that a long time ago!

Baseball Player: Son, would you please get my fielder's glove out of the car?

Son (Later): Dad, I can't find it!

Player: Where did you look?

Son: In the glove compartment!

Louie: I came home early from baseball practice because I didn't want to get sick.

Mother: What do you mean?

Louie: I told the coach I wanted to be the catcher, and he told me the only thing I'll ever catch is a cold!

Little Boy: How many fish have you caught, Mister?

Fisherman: None yet, but I've only been fishing for an hour.

Little Boy: That's better than the man who was fishing here yesterday.

Fisherman: How is it better?

Little Boy: It took him five hours to do what you've done in just one!

Linda: Want to come watch our game? We're the champions so far.

Katie: Are you really?

Linda: Sure, it's our first game of the season!

Rookie Player: What does it take to hit a ball the way you do?

Veteran Ballplayer: A bat.

Q: What did the bucking bronco say to his rider at the rodeo?

A: "Get off my back!"

Jerry: My brother makes about 15 baskets a day.

Ginny: Is he a basket weaver?

Jerry: No, he's a basketball player!

Ronnie: Shh! I'm hunting for lions!

Donnie: There are no lions here.

Ronnie: If there were, I wouldn't have to hunt for them.

Q: What kind of dog is a fighter?

A: A Boxer.

Umpire: I have to admit, the kids on your team are good losers.

Coach: Good? They're perfect!

Jimmy: Mom, will you please give me a dollar for a man who's crying in the ballpark?

Mom: What's he crying about?

Jimmy: He's crying, "Hot dogs, one dollar!"

Dick: According to my watch, I can run 100 yards in 10 seconds.

Rick: My watch runs slow, too.

Julie: My father went hunting, and he shot three ducks.

Sam: Were they wild?

Julie: No, but the farmer who owned the them was.

Tom: Look what I caught! A jellyfish!

Ron: Really? What flavor?

Eddie: Mommy, I just found a lost football.

Mommy: How do you know it's lost?

Eddie: Because the kids down the street are still looking for it!

Cathy: How do you make a fisherman's net?

Patsy: Just sew a lot of holes together!

Coach: Why do you think you'll make a good football player?

Student: Because I've got athlete's feet!

First Little League Manager: Your team made more errors than any team I've ever seen! You should have left half your team home.

Second Manager: I did.

Child (at first baseball game): Dad, why is that man running?

Father: Because he hit the ball.

Child: Is he afraid he's going to get spanked?

Boy: What kind of fish is that?

Fisherman: Smelt.

Boy: Sure does. But what kind of fish is it?

Q: What kind of dishes do baseball players have?

A: Home plates.

Q: Why is it always cool in a football stadium?

A: Because it's full of fans.

Ellen: Do you know what Lisa did after she won the swimming meet?

Jennie: No, what did she do?

Ellen: She dried herself off!

Mother: Nancy, why don't you play tennis with Freddy anymore?

Nancy: Would you play with someone who keeps lying about the score?

Mother: Certainly not!

Nancy: Neither would Freddy!

Georgie: I was down at the lake and I saw a catfish.

Porgie: Did it catch anything?

First Camper: Did you clean that fish before you put it into the frying pan?

Second Camper: What for? I just pulled it out of the water.

Mother: Why are you home so early from practice?

Susie: I just got bored playing left.

Mother: Left field?

Susie: No, left out.

Billy: Boy, am I glad I'm not a fish.

Willy: Why?

Billy: Because they spend all their time in schools!

Q: Where is the biggest diamond in the world?

A: Yankee Stadium.

Q: How do witches play baseball?

A: They use their bats.

Barney: I'm taking a course in parachute jumping.

Arnie: How many jumps do you have to make before you pass the course?

Barney: All of them!

Ross: I went crab fishing, and a crab bit off one of my toes.

Ann: Which one?

Ross: How should I know? All crabs look alike.

Helen: I bet I can tell you the score of this soccer game before it starts.

Ellen: Okay, smartie, tell me.

Helen: Nothing to nothing.

Q: What do eggs and a losing ball team have in common?

A: They both get beaten.

Q: What do quarterbacks like on their sandwiches?

A: Pass-trami.

Q: Who brings presents to basketball players at Christmas?

A: Center Claus.

Q: What has 18 legs and flies?

A: A baseball team.

Swimmer: Are there any alligators in this swamp?

Swamp Dweller: I don't think so. The sharks scare them away!

Mike: I can't go swimming right now. I just ate, and my mother said I shouldn't swim on a full stomache.

Rosie: Then swim on your back!

First Hunter: I just ran into a big bear!

Second Hunter: Did you let him have both barrels?

First Hunter: Heck, I let him have the whole gun!

Liz: I had to quit the basketball team because the coach got sick.

Diz: What does that have to do with your quitting the team?

Liz: She got sick of watching me play.

Q: What did one fish say to another fish after it was hooked?

A: "That's what you get for not keeping your mouth shut."

Q: What did the ballplayer get for hitting the ball out of the park?

A: A home run.

Dennis: Timmy isn't our quarterback anymore because of his mother.

Harvey: Why? What did she do?

Dennis: She told him not to pass anything until somebody said, "Please."

Q: What did one football say to another?

A: "People get a kick out of me!"

Ann: Sally, how come you're catching so many fish and I'm not catching any?

Sally: I don't know. I guess your worm just isn't trying hard enough.

Baseball Manager to Outfielder: You've been missing a lot of balls out there. If you can't do any better, I'm going to have to put another player in the outfield!

Outfielder: Gee, thanks! I sure could use some extra help.

Two kids were fishing. A younger kid came by and watched them.

Younger Kid: What are you guys doing? Fishing?

Older Kid: No, we're drowning worms.

Penny: I just saw a man eating shark!

Denny: Where?

Penny: In the restaurant at the end of the pier!

Bobby: I fell down a dozen times while ice-skating today.

Jeff: Did anyone make any funny cracks?

Bobby: Only the ice.

Q: A girl was hit in the head at a baseball game. Guess what came out of her mouth?

A: A bawl.

Gym Teacher to Boxer: Stay down till nine!

Boxer: I can't! I've got another class at 8:30!

Arnie (pulling fish out of water): This fish sure must be happy to be caught!

Barnie: What makes you think so?

Arnie: Look how it's wagging its tail.

Umpire: Hey, kid, that was only strike two. You have another one coming.

Batter: I don't want it!

Sherry: What's the difference between a strike and a ball?

Jerry: I don't know.

Sherry: Okay, then you can be umpire for our game.

Artie: Why do you keep falling down? Can't you ice-skate?

Marty: I'm not sure. I've never been on my feet long enough to find out!

Some neighborhood kids were playing football. Leo kept fumbling the ball.

Paul: That Leo is terrible! Why do we let him play on our team?

Emily: We've got to. It's his ball!

Judy: My dad just came back from hunting man-eating tigers.

Trudy: Did he have any luck?

Judy: He sure did. He never came across any!

Hunter: Say, have you seen a deer around here?

Farmer: Yes.

Hunter: How long ago?

Farmer: About a year.

Jerry: My dad went hunting with our neighbor, and he shot this stuffed tiger.

Terry: What's it stuffed with?

Jerry: Our neighbor.

Game Warden: You kids can't fish without a permit!

Chris: Not so. We're using worms, and the fish are biting like crazy!

Betty fell into the lake while fishing. A man passed by and helped her out of the water.

Man: How'd you come to fall in?

Betty: I didn't. I came to fish.

Man in Fish Market: Throw me a fish!

Fish Market Clerk: What for?

Man: So I can show my family the fish I caught!

Jan: Why are you swimming with your coat on?

Ann: Because the water's cold!

Q: What do a bat and a flyswatter have in common?

A: They both hit flies.

Q: Why didn't a single man get a hit at a baseball game?

A: Because only married men played!

Fred: How's the fishing around here?

Ned: It's okay.

Fred: Then how come you haven't caught any fish?

Ned: You asked me about fishing, not catching.

Q: Who can go as fast as a race horse?

A: The jockey.

Mother: Billy, I don't want you to play with anyone who cheats or steals.

Billy: Does that mean I can't play with Henry next door?

Mother: Why not? Does he cheat?

Billy: No, but we played baseball yesterday, and he stole second base!

Q: Where do hungry football players play?

A: In the Supper Bowl.

Q: What kind of ends do you find in libraries?

A: Bookends.

Q: What do you call a sweaty basketball player?

A: A hot shot.

Q: Where are the most outs made in baseball?

A: In the outfield.

This book is available in two editions:
Library binding by Carolrhoda Books, Inc.,
   a division of Lerner Publishing Group
Soft cover by First Avenue Editions,
   an imprint of Lerner Publishing Group
241 First Avenue North
Minneapolis, MN 55401

Website address: www.lernerbooks.com

Library of Congress Cataloging-in-Publication Data

Schultz, Sam.
     Game-day gigglers : winning jokes to score some laughs / by Sam Schultz ;
pictures by Brian Gable.
        p.   cm. — (Make me laugh)
     Summary: A collection of jokes about sports and games.
     ISBN: 1−57505−644−5 (lib. bdg. : alk. paper)
     ISBN: 1−57505−706−9 (pbk. : alk. paper)
     1. Sports—Juvenile humor. [1. Sports—Humor. 2. Jokes. 3. Riddles. 4. Puns
and punning.] I. Gable, Brian, 1949− ill. II. Title. III. Series.
PN6231.S65 S34 2004
818'.5402—dc21   2002151103

Manufactured in the United States of America
1 2 3 4 5 6 − DP − 09 08 07 06 05 04